DATE DUE

SE 15 00			

DEMCO 38-297

YOU'D *never* BELIEVE IT BUT...

flies can taste with their feet

and other facts about senses

BANNOCKBURN SCHOOL DIST. 106
2165 TELEGRAPH ROAD
DEERFIELD, ILLINOIS 60015

Designed and produced by
Aladdin Books Ltd
28 Percy Street
London W1P 0LD

*First published in the United States
in 1998 by*
Copper Beech Books,
an imprint of
The Millbrook Press
2 Old New Milford Road
Brookfield, Connecticut 06804

Designed by
David West Children's Book Design
Designer
Flick Killerby
Computer illustrations
Stephen Sweet (Simon Girling & Associates)
Picture Research
Brooks Krikler Research
Project Editor
Sally Hewitt
Editor
Jon Richards

Printed in Belgium

Library of Congress Cataloging-in-Publication Data
Taylor, Helen (Helen Suzanne), 1963-
Flies can taste with their feet and other amazing facts
about senses / by Helen Taylor ; illustrated by Stephen
Sweet.
p. cm. — (You'd never believe it but—)
Includes index.
Summary: Presents facts about the five senses, including
information about how plants and animals sense their
surroundings.
ISBN 0-7613-0861-X (lib. bdg.)
1. Senses and sensation—Juvenile literature.
[1. Senses and sensation.] I. Sweet, Stephen,
1965- ill. II. Title. III. Series.
QP434.T39 1998   98-4268
573.8'7—dc21   CIP AC
5 4 3 2 1

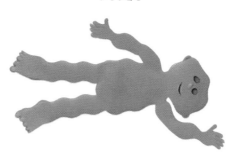

YOU'D *never* BELIEVE IT BUT...

flies can taste with their feet

and other facts about senses

Helen Taylor

COPPER BEECH BOOKS
BROOKFIELD, CONNECTICUT

Contents

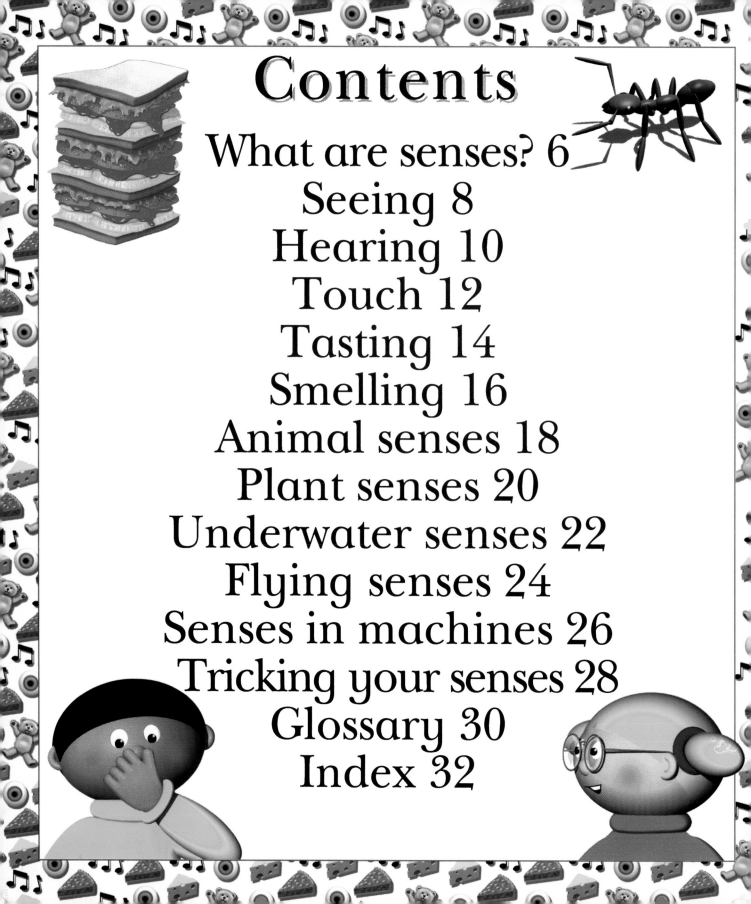

Introduction

Colors, flavors, sounds, and smells — you will sense all of these every day.
Your body is covered with thousands and thousands of tiny sensors that help you to see, touch, taste, smell, and hear the world around you. Join Jack and Jo as they discover all about senses, from how a bat "sees" in the dark to how you taste your food.

FUN PROJECT
Wherever you see this sign, it means there is a fun project that you can do.

Each project will help you to understand more about the subject. You'd never believe it but... each project is fun to do!

What are senses?

You have five main senses. These let you see, hear, feel, smell, and taste what is going on in the world all around you. You probably don't think about it much, but you use your senses all the time.

Look at Jack and Jo. They can hear each other talking. What else do you think they can hear? What do you think they can see, feel, and smell? Are they tasting anything?

> Can you see the haunted house?

You'd never believe it but...

Newborn babies can tell who their mother is by using their sense of smell.

Your eyes, ears, skin, nose, and tongue
are your five main sense organs.
They pick up information from
the world around you about
colors, sounds, shapes
and textures, smells,
and tastes.

No, but I can
hear it!

USING YOUR SENSES
Make yourself a sandwich
with your favorite filling. Use
your eyes. What can you see?
Touch the sandwich with your
fingers. What can you feel with your
skin? Use your nose. What can you
smell? Take a bite
and munch. What
can you taste with
your tongue? Use
your ears. What
can you hear?

Seeing

Your eyes are the sense organs you use for seeing. They are always receiving information about the world around you. Your eyes can see many different shapes and colors as well as things moving.

You recognize people and know what things are because your brain makes a picture from the signals sent to it by your eyes.

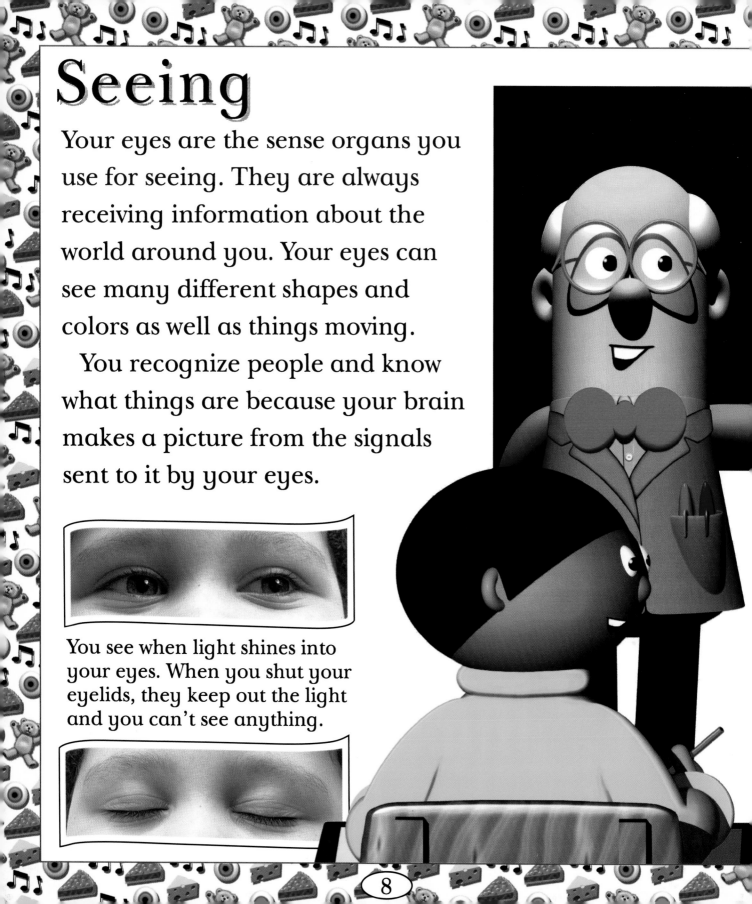

You see when light shines into your eyes. When you shut your eyelids, they keep out the light and you can't see anything.

Many people wear glasses or contact lenses to improve their eyesight.

You'd never believe it but...

You have a hole in the middle of your eye! The black spot in your eye is really a hole called a pupil. The colored iris can make the pupil bigger or smaller to let more or less light into your eye.

I can read much better with my glasses on.

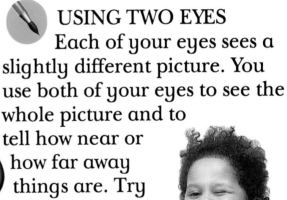

USING TWO EYES
Each of your eyes sees a slightly different picture. You use both of your eyes to see the whole picture and to tell how near or how far away things are. Try catching a ball with both eyes open. Now shut one eye and try again. Which is easier?

Hearing

Your ears are amazing. They let you hear all kinds of different sounds. You can hear your friends talking, music playing, a loud crash of thunder, and a soft whisper. What sounds do you like to hear? Stop and listen. What sounds can you hear? Do you recognize them?

As well as letting us hear, our ears help us to keep our balance.

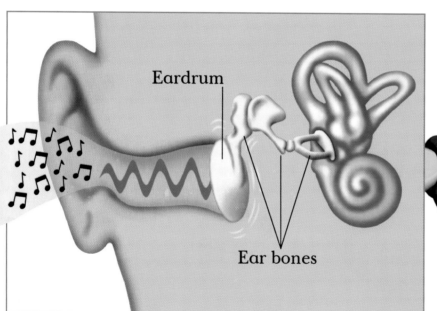

Eardrum

Ear bones

Can you play that quietly?

You'd never believe it but...

Your ear has a drum! Sounds make your eardrum vibrate. This makes three bones vibrate and they wobble a liquid. This wobbling sends signals to the brain and you hear the sound.

When you clap your hands, the air around your hands shake very fast. Each shake is called a vibration. These vibrations travel through the air as sound.

Ears are a special shape for hearing. They trap sound vibrations and send them inside your ear.

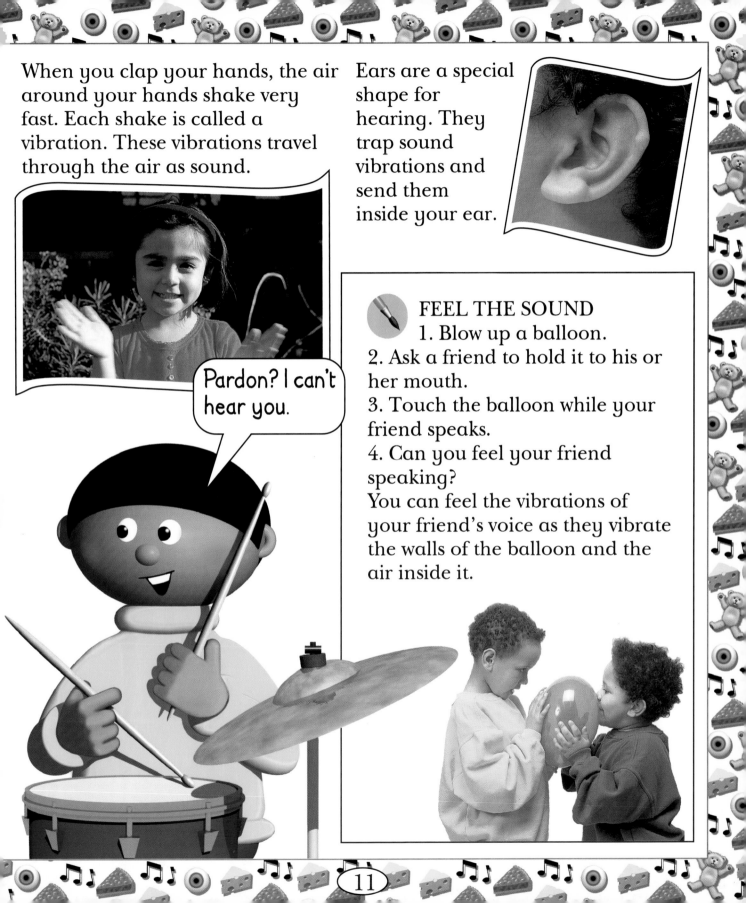

Pardon? I can't hear you.

FEEL THE SOUND
1. Blow up a balloon.
2. Ask a friend to hold it to his or her mouth.
3. Touch the balloon while your friend speaks.
4. Can you feel your friend speaking?

You can feel the vibrations of your friend's voice as they vibrate the walls of the balloon and the air inside it.

Touch

The skin that covers your body is full of tiny sensors. These send lots of different messages to your brain about things that touch your body.

When you touch something, you feel if it is hard or soft, or if it is hot or cold or wet or dry.

Smooth, rough, tickly, and bumpy are some words that describe the way things feel. What other feeling words do you know?

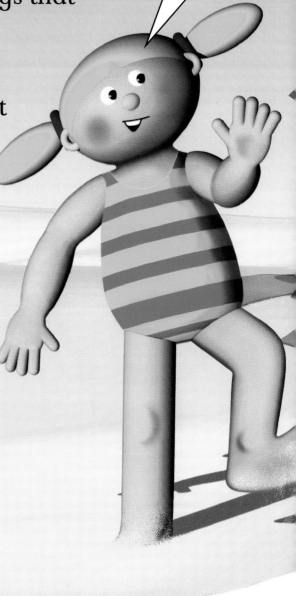

I can feel warm sand between my toes.

You'd never believe it but...

If the skin that covers your body was laid out flat, it would stretch over the same area as a large beach towel!

Yuk, this seaweed feels cold and slimy.

The skin on the tips of your fingers is very good for feeling. When you want to find out what something feels like, you usually touch it with your fingertips.

GUESSING THE DISTANCE

Close your eyes and get a friend to gently run their finger up your arm. Try to stop them when you think they are near your elbow crease. How close were you?

Tasting

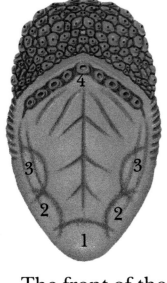

Look at your tongue in the mirror. Does it look rough? It probably feels rough too. This is because it is covered in thousands of taste buds. The tiny taste buds detect whether food tastes sweet like cake, salty like a bag of potato chips, sour like a lemon, or bitter like vinegar.

The front of the tongue (1) tastes sweet things. Behind this is the salty area (2), and farther back is the sour area (3). At the back of the tongue is the area that tastes bitter things (4).

Do you want a taste of this bun? It's really sweet.

TASTING COLOR

Candy makers sometimes give candy a color that suggests a flavor. For example, a lemon-flavored candy might have a yellow color and a lime-flavored candy might have a green color. See if you can guess the flavor of some candy just by looking at its color.

No thanks. I prefer this salty popcorn.

You'd never believe it but...

Babies and young children have a better sense of taste than grown-ups because they have taste buds on the inside of their cheeks as well as their tongues.

Smelling

There are tiny amounts of "smelly" chemicals in the air all around you. You can't see them but your nose can sense them. When you sniff air up your nose, the smelly chemicals hit smell detectors right at the top of your nose. The smell detectors send messages to your brain.

If something is dirty or full of germs it can smell bad. The bad smell is a warning that it could make you sick.

I can smell those cheeses from here!

You'd never believe it but...

You can put smells in a bottle. People spend lots of money on perfumes to make themselves smell nice.

This fruit smells lovely.

USING YOUR NOSE

Peel and cut an apple and a pear into the same size pieces. Get someone to blindfold you. Hold your nose and eat one of the pieces. See if you can guess which one is which. Is it easier to tell which is which when you don't hold your nose?

Animal senses

Animals have the same five senses as you do, but their senses can work very differently from yours. Animals that are hunted, like hares, often have eyes on the sides of their heads. These let them see all around and look out for enemies that might be hunting them for food.

Cats hunt at night so they need to be able to see when it is very dark. They have large eyes that let in as much light as possible.

Why is Sam running to you?

Dogs have very sharp senses of smell and hearing. They can hear and smell things that we cannot. Watch out for how dogs prick up their ears and sniff to find out what is going on.

You'd never believe it but...

Flies can taste with their feet. They have special sensors on their feet that let them know if they have landed on something that is good to eat.

He can smell his food.

SMELLY TRAILS

Ants have a sense of smell. Have you ever seen ants follow each other in a line? Ants leave a smelly trail of chemicals for other ants to follow. They also use their antennae to sense what's going on around them.

Plant senses

Plants do not have eyes, ears, noses, tongues, and skin like you, but they are still sensitive to the world around them. Plants cannot see, but can sense where light is coming from. They grow toward the light, even if it means growing around corners.

Some flowers are so sensitive to light that they open their petals during the day and close them at night.

All the sunflowers are facing the same way.

Plants with floppy stems, like sweet peas, put out tendrils. These wave around until they find something to wrap around and support the plant.

You'd never believe it but...

Bladderworts grow underwater. When a tiny creature bumps into the plant, a bladder opens up and sucks the creature in for food.

Yes, they follow the sun.

FINDING LIGHT

Put a houseplant near a window and watch it grow toward the light. Turn the plant around and see how it will grow back toward the light again.

Gravity is a force that pulls everything downward. Roots always grow downward because they are sensitive to the pull of gravity.

Underwater senses

Underwater creatures use their senses to help them to hunt for food and to live safely in the water. Did you know that there are smells and sounds underwater?

Sharks are so sensitive that they can "feel" the heartbeat of another fish. They also have a strong sense of smell, which they use to hunt for food.

No, but if we were in the water, he could smell us.

Can the shark see us?

BANNOCKBURN SCHOOL DIST. 106
2165 TELEGRAPH ROAD
DEERFIELD, ILLINOIS 60015

Schools of fish never collide with each other. They have sensitive organs that can feel when another fish is swimming nearby.

Parts of the ocean are so deep that no light reaches there. Many deep-sea fish have lights on their bodies. Angler fish grow their own fishing rod with a light on the end. This light attracts smaller fish, which the angler fish catches and eats.

You'd never believe it but...

The song of a blue whale is the loudest sound produced by any living thing. Whales talk to each other using sounds that travel a long way through the water. These sounds can hurt human ears if they swim too close to whales.

Flying senses

Birds of prey flying high in the air need very sharp eyesight to spot food far below. An eagle is a bird of prey. When it spies a small animal moving on the ground, it swoops down and catches it in its talons, the strong claws on its feet.

You'd never believe it but...

The circles of feathers around an owl's eyes do not help it to see. They catch sounds so that the owl can hear better when it is hunting.

How does the bat see in the dark?

The world is made up of lots of different colors. Collect some colored, see-through candy wrappers and look through them. Looking through the candy wrappers will make things appear to change color.

Bats make very high squeaks as they fly. These sounds bounce back off insects, like an echo, and the bats can hear exactly where the insects are.

He uses his ears to "see."

You can see millions of shades of colors, but birds can see even more colors than you. Many male birds display brightly colored feathers to attract a mate.

Senses in machines

You use your sense organs to detect what is going on around you and to decide what to do next. Did you know that machines can do something very similar? Some machines can hear sounds, called ultrasound waves. These are too high for you to hear. When you walk up to an automatic door in a supermarket, it senses you coming and opens up to let you in.

Some televisions can see light that you cannot see. It is called infrared light. Remote controls send a beam of infrared light to the television that tells it to turn on or change channels.

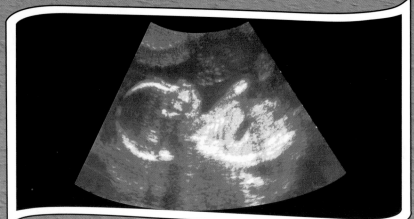

You'd never believe it but...

We can see pictures of a baby while it is still inside the mother. An ultrasound machine sends out sound waves that bounce off the baby. The machine forms a picture from the echoes that bounce off the baby.

Why can't I change channels?

I'm in the way of the beam.

SEEING HEAT
Rub your hands together until they feel hot. Now quickly hold your hands up against a mirror. Can you see the warm, moist air from your hands misting up the mirror?

A burglar alarm can tell if there is a person nearby by sensing heat made by a human body. If the alarm feels heat from someone walking by, it turns on and sounds the alarm.

Tricking your senses

Sometimes your eyes play tricks on you. You cannot always believe what you see! Every time you watch a movie, your eyes are playing a trick on you. You think you are seeing something moving, when really you are looking at thousands of still pictures.

TRICK YOUR TASTE
Eat a piece of an orange, then eat a mint closely followed by another piece of the orange. How different does the second piece of the orange taste after the mint?

I've got a hole in my hand!

SEE-THROUGH HAND
Roll a piece of paper up into a tube. With one eye, look through the tube at something on the other side of the room. Cover the other eye with the palm of your hand, but keep your eye open. Now move this hand away from your eye, down the side of the tube. What do you see? Have you really got a hole in your hand?

You'd never believe it but...

Some people throw their voice. Ventriloquists can talk without moving their lips, making you believe that their dummy is speaking.

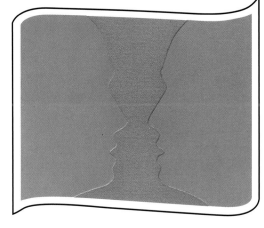

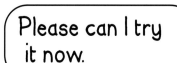

Please can I try it now.

We can draw pictures that trick our sense of sight. Is this a picture of two faces talking to each other, or is it a picture of a vase?

Many animals are specially colored to hide themselves from other animals. This spider has hidden on a flower and is waiting for an unsuspecting fly to catch and eat!

Glossary

Brain

Your brain sits inside your head and is protected by your hard, bony skull. The brain lets you see, hear, feel, smell, and taste and make sense of things happening around you.

Detect

To detect means to find out or discover. Your senses help you to be a detective. For example, your nose detects smells and your ears detect sounds.

Ears

Your ears are the sense organs that collect all kinds of different sounds. They turn these sounds into signals that are then sent to your brain. The brain then tells you what kind of sounds you are hearing.

Eyes

Your eyes are the sense organs that detect shades of light and dark, as well as colors, shapes, and movement. Messages are sent from your eyes to your brain and your brain tells you what you are seeing in front of you.

Gravity

Gravity is a natural force. The gravity of the earth pulls everything downward. When you throw an object up in the air, it always falls down again.

Iris

The iris is the colored circle in your eye that sits around the pupil in the center. It opens and closes to let more or less light into the eye.

Nose

Your nose is your sense organ that detects different smells. When you take a sniff, you can sense all kinds of different smells in the air.

Pupil

The pupil is the black spot in the center of your eye. It is really a hole that lets light into your eyes so that you can see.

Sense organs

Your sense organs are your eyes, ears, nose, tongue, and skin. They are the parts of your body that let you detect light, color, and movement, sound, smells, tastes, and what things feel like.

Senses

You have five senses — sight, hearing, smell, taste, and touch. Your senses tell you what is happening around you.

Skin

Your skin is your sense organ that detects what the things you touch feel like. Your brain tells you whether things are hot or cold, sharp or blunt, rough or smooth.

Tongue

Your tongue is your sense organ that detects different tastes. The surface of your tongue is covered with small taste pits. Inside these taste pits are even smaller taste buds. These detect whether the food or drink you eat is sweet, salty, sour, or bitter.

Ultrasound waves

Ultrasound waves are sounds that are too high for people to hear. Some animals and some specially designed machines can sense ultrasound waves.

Index

A
air 11, 16, 24, 27
antennae 19

B
balance 10
bones 10, 30
brains 8, 10, 12, 16, 30, 31

C
colors 5, 7, 8, 15, 25, 29, 30, 31

E
ears 7, 10, 11, 18, 20, 23, 25, 30, 31
echoes 25, 26
eyes 7, 8, 9, 18, 20, 24, 28, 30, 31

F
feel 6, 7, 12, 13, 22, 23, 27, 30, 31
flavors 5, 15
flowers 20, 21, 29
flying 24, 25
food 5, 14, 15, 18, 19, 21, 22, 24

H
hearing 5, 6, 7, 10, 11, 18, 24, 25, 26, 30, 31

L
light 8, 9, 18, 20, 21, 23, 26, 30

N
noses 7, 16, 17, 20, 30, 31

S
sight 5, 6, 7, 8, 27, 29, 30, 31
skin 7, 12, 13, 20, 31
smell 5, 6, 7, 16, 17, 18, 19, 22, 30, 31
sounds 5, 7, 10, 11, 23, 24, 25, 26, 30, 31

T
taste 5, 6, 7, 14, 15, 17, 19, 28, 30, 31
tongues 7, 14, 15, 20, 31
taste buds 14, 15, 31
touch 5, 12, 13

U
ultrasound waves 26, 31

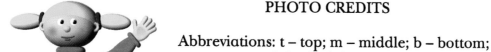

PHOTO CREDITS

Abbreviations: t – top; m – middle; b – bottom; r – right; l – left; c – center.

All the photography in this book is by Roger Vlitos except the following pages:
Pages 6-7 & 29tr – Pictor International. 17, 24 both, 25 & 29tl – Frank Spooner Pictures. 18, 20 both, 21 & 23 both – Bruce Coleman Collection. 19, 26 & 27 – Science Photo Library.